CHOY LI FUT KUNG-FU

by
Doc Fai Wong
and
Jane Hallander

To the late Grandmaster Lau Bun, my first choy li fut teacher; and to my teachers in Hong Kong, Grandmasters Woo Van Cheuk, Wong Gong, and Wong Ying Sum, who greatly expanded my knowledge.

I am also grateful to my si-hing (senior classmate), Master M. L. Jew, for first encouraging me to open a choy li fut school in San Francisco.

DISCLAIMER

Please note that the publisher of this instructional book is NOT RESPONSIBLE in any manner whatsoever for any injury which may occur by reading and/or following the instructions herein.

It is essential that before following any of the activities, physical or otherwise, herein described, the reader or readers should first consult his or her physician for advice on whether or not the reader or readers should embark on the physical activity described herein. Since the physical activities described herein may be too sophisticated in nature, it is *essential that a physician be consulted.*

UP UNIQUE PUBLICATIONS

Unique Publications
4201 Vanowen Place
Burbank, CA 91505

ISBN: 0-86568-062-0
Library of Congress Catalog Card Number: 84-32683

Contents

Introduction

The name *choy li fut* has been spelled in several different ways. One spelling is choy *lay* fut, where *lay* is the standard Cantonese sound for the proper name "Li." Choy *lee* fut is another spelling commonly seen. In this instance, *lee* is another way to spell the name "Li."

The *li* in choy li fut comes from the kung-fu style of Li Yau-San. His last name can be spelled *Li* or *Lee*, but no one spells that last name *lay*. *Li* is used in this book, rather than *lee*, because most United States publications spell that last name *Li*.

In Hong Kong, some martial arts associations use these spellings: *choi, lee,* or *fat*. *Fat* is used because, in Hong Kong, the people pronounce *fut* as *fat*. Correct pronunciation is *fut* (as in *but*).

Choy is sometimes spelled *tsoi*. That is a different Romanization of the family name which is spelled *Choy* in the United States.

Choy li fut in Mandarin Romanization is spelled *tsai li fo*. However, since choy li fut is a Southern Chinese system, we use the Cantonese pronunciation and Romanization.

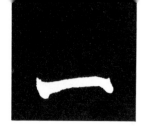

History of Choy Li Fut

Although known as a Southern system, choy li fut kung-fu has its origins in both Northern and Southern China. The system's founder, Chan Heung, had three teachers, two from the South and one from the North. Choy li fut is one of the few kung-fu styles that is strongly influenced by both Northern and Southern Chinese kung-fu, combining the long arm techniques of the South with the quick agile footwork that characterizes Northern China's martial arts.

Choy li fut was founded in 1836 by Chan Heung, a well-known and highly-skilled martial artist of that period. Also known as Din Ying, Chan Heung was born in 1806, in King Mui, a village in the San Wui district of Kwangtung province. His martial arts career began at age seven, when he went to live with his uncle, Yuen Woo.

Yuen Woo was a famous boxer from the legendary Shaolin temple. From Yuen Woo, Chan Heung learned the art of Shaolin kung-fu, and became so proficient at it that by age fifteen he could defeat any challenger from nearby villages.

By the time he reached his seventeenth year, Chan Heung was ready to assimilate more martial skills. So Yuen Woo took him to Li Yau-San, Yuen's senior classmate from the Shaolin temple. Chan Heung spent the next four years perfecting his kung-fu under Li Yau-San's careful eye.

It was apparent to Li Yau-San that after only four years of training, Chan Heung was again ready to move on to higher levels. In ten years, he had already reached a level in kung-fu that had taken Yuen Woo and Li Yau-San twenty years to attain.

Li Yau-San suggested a Shaolin monk who lived as a recluse on Lau Fu mountain as the best teacher for Chan Heung. The only problem was that the monk, Choy Fok, no longer wished to teach martial arts. He wanted only to be left alone to cultivate Buddhism.

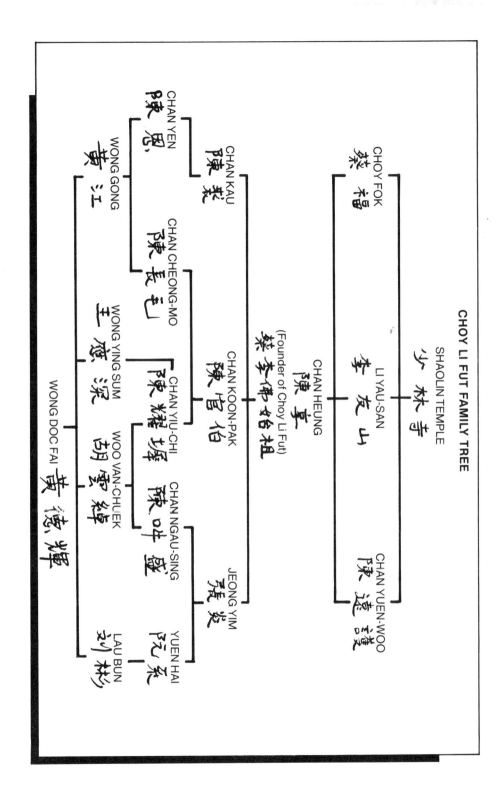

CHOY LI FUT FAMILY TREE

SHAOLIN TEMPLE
少林寺

CHOY FOK
蔡福

LI YAU-SAN
李友山

CHAN YUEN-WOO
陳遠護

CHAN HEUNG
陳享
(Founder of Choy Li Fut)
蔡李佛始祖

CHAN YEN
陳恩

CHAN KAU
陳九

WONG GONG
黃江

CHAN CHEONG-MO
陳長毛

CHAN KOON-PAK
陳官伯

CHAN NGAU-SING
陳牛

JEONG YIM
張炎

WONG YING SUM
王隱深

CHAN YIU-CHI
陳耀墀

CHAN NGAU-SING
陳牛

YUEN HAI
阮系

LAU BUN
劉林

WONG DOC FAI
黃德輝

WOO VAN-CHUEK
胡雲綽

WONG YING SUM
王隱深

3

Realizing that reaching his highest potential in kung-fu meant finding the monk and becoming his disciple, Chan Heung set out on the long trek to Lau Fu mountain.

Choy Fok's head had been seriously burned when he took his Buddhist vows and had healed with ugly scars. This gave him the nickname "Monk with the Wounded Head." Armed with that knowledge, Chan Heung sought out anyone on Lau Fu mountain who could help him find Choy Fok. Finally, he located the monk, and handed him a letter of recommendation from Li Yau-San. After waiting patiently to be accepted as Choy Fok's disciple, he was stunned when Choy Fok turned him down.

After much begging from Chan Heung, Choy Fok agreed to take the young man as a student—but only to study Buddhism. So, Chan Heung studied Buddhism for many hours a day with the monk of the scarred head, and practiced his martial arts by himself, far into the night.

Early one morning, Chan Heung was practicing his kung-fu, sweeping both legs across heavy bamboo bush and kicking up stones, then smashing them to pieces before they hit the ground. Suddenly, the monk appeared and asked him if that were the best he could do. Chan Heung was shocked when Choy Fok pointed to a large rock weighing about eighty pounds and told him to kick it twelve feet. Bracing himself, Chan Heung exerted all of his strength as his foot crashed against the rock, sending it barely twelve feet away. Instead of giving the expected compliment, Choy Fok placed his own foot under the heavy rock and effortlessly propelled it through the air. Chan Heung was awestruck by this demonstration of "superpower." Again he begged Choy Fok to take him as a martial arts disciple. This time the monk agreed, and for eight years Choy Fok taught Chan Heung both the way of Buddhism and the way of martial arts.

When he was twenty-nine, Chan Heung left the monk and went back to King Mui village, where he spent the next two years revising and refining all that he had learned from Choy Fok. Chan Heung had now developed a new system of kung-fu. In 1836 he formally established the choy li fut system, naming it in honor of two of his teachers, Choy Fok and Li Yau-San, and used the word *fut*, which means "Buddha" in Chinese, to pay homage to his uncle, Yuen Woo, and to the Shaolin roots of the new system.

Chan Heung set up a martial arts school in the local temple of his village to teach the new system. As his reputation spread, hundreds of people from nearby villages came to learn choy li fut.

Shortly after Chang Heung established his new school, the Opium Wars broke out in China. Like many other loyal Chinese, Chan Heung joined the army in Canton to fight against the British invaders. Following China's defeat in 1842, he returned home to his family.

Political corruption from within the Manchurian-controlled Ching dynasty had contributed to China's defeat. Between 1847 and 1850 many Chinese leaders formed secret societies to combat the evil forces of the Ching. Under the leadership of Hung Hsiu-Chuen, the Triad Rebellion broke out against the Imperial forces in Kwangsi. Hung's rebels defeated the government troops in 1850 and for the next two decades the Tai Ping Tien Kuo kingdom ruled China.

During the rebellion, Chan Heung's followers urged him to join in the revolt. However, he was a devout Buddhist and shunned the path of violence. Nevertheless, he continued to train his followers in case the need arose to do battle against the corrupt Ching rulers.

When the Imperial army sought to recruit men from his area to fight against the rebel forces, Chan Heung left his home in King Mui with his wife and two children. Finally forced by the needless fighting and destruction to participate actively, he set up many choy li fut schools in Southern China to spread revolutionary ideas against the Manchurians. He gave his followers a special signal for future battlefield reunions: Whoever belonged to the choy li fut system would cry out "yak" when striking with his fist, "wak" when thrusting with a tiger claw hand, and "dik" when kicking.

When the Tai Ping Tien Kuo succumbed in 1864, Chan Heung left China. At age fifty-nine he became the martial arts teacher for the Chan Family Association overseas. He stayed abroad four years, and then returned home to King Mui, where he was able to see his own kung-fu system gain tremendous popularity throughout Southern China.

On August 20, 1875, at the age of sixty-nine, Chan Heung died. He was buried in his beloved village of King Mui. But his memory lives on, perpetuated in the kung-fu system that he established.

After Chan Heung's death, his choy li fut legacy passed on to his two sons, Chan On-Pak and Chan Koon-Pak. Chan On-Pak, born in 1839 and the older of the two brothers, looked like and had the gentle nature of a scholar. His specialty was the spear. Chan On-Pak's control of the spear was so advanced that he gained the nickname *yet cheung ng mui fa* or "five blossoms with one lance."

Chan Koon-Pak

In 1894, two of Chan On-Pak's students, Cheng Si Leung and Chan Siu Bak, helped the revolutionary forces of Sun Yat-Sen fight against the Ching dynasty and lay the foundation of the Republic of China.

The younger son, Chan Koon-Pak, left King Mui to become a merchant in Kong Moon City, where his fame as a martial artist spread quickly. He soon had no time to spend as a merchant and devoted all of his efforts teaching choy li fut. Chan Koon-Pak later established a large choy li fut training center in Canton City.

Chan Heung had eighteen original choy li fut disciples. In 1848, the original eighteen started branching out to teach choy li fut throughout Southern China. The first disciple to teach choy li fut outside of King Mui was Lung Ji Choi, who opened a kung-fu school in the village of Chum Jao in Kwangsi province. Soon after, Chan Din Yao and Chan Din Fune initiated the first choy li fut school in Fut San.

Other of the original eighteen disciples who promoted the new kung-fu system were: Chan Dai Yup in Kwang Chow; Chan Din Sing in Chung San; Chan Mau Jong in Poon Yu; Chan Din

Chan Yui-Chi

Bong in Tung Kong; Chan Din Wai in Hoi Ping; Chan Din Jen in Toi San; Chan Sun Dong in Yen Ping; Chan Din Duk at Hok San; Chan Dai Wai in Siu Hing; Chan Sing Hin in Sun Wui City; Chan Yin Yu at Gong Moon. And admirable tasks were performed by Chan Dai Sing, Chan Din Sing, Chan Mau Wing, and Chan Din Gung, who taught choy li fut in twenty-six villages in the King Mui area.

In 1867, another student of Chan Heung's, Jeong Yim, journeyed to Fut San to reopen the school originally established by Chan Din Yao and Chan Din Fune. Jeong Yim became known as the "father of the hung sing school of choy li fut."

It is generally thought that there are two schools of choy li fut: hung sing and bak sing, and that there are two representatives of the hung sing school. During the revolution of the mid-1800s,

Young Doc Fai Wong and his late teacher, Woo Van Cheuk and the great-grand-daughter of Choy Li Fut's founder, Chan Heung, Ms. Chan Kit Fong (1976)

the Hung Moon Party represented all revolutionary factions, including choy li fut representatives. Choy li fut schools had a secret slogan during these times: "*Hung* ying ji *sing;* ying *hung* wing *sing.*" This translates as: "heroes of the Hung Party are superior; heroes always win."

Chan Heung's followers adopted two words of the motto as their secret passwords—hung sing—which meant "Hung Party wins." But, because that was too close to the outlawed Hung Moon Party name, they changed it to another slogan which sounds the same as *hung sing,* but means "goose winning."

Meanwhile, the Fut San Choy Li Fut School of Jeong Yim bore the name "hung sing kwoon" (using the "hung" that means goose). Some of his students began referring to him as Jeong Hung Sing. By the time his school had developed a third generation of students, the true meaning of "hung sing" had been lost, and his third generation students believed him to be the founder of a type of choy li fut known as hung sing choy li fut.

To clarify the issue, Chan Heung's son, Koon-Pak, changed the name hung sing to a different *hung* meaning "strong." From that time on, choy li fut schools in Koon-Pak's King Mui area designated themselves with the slogan *hung sing,* meaning "strong winning," while the fut san schools kept their "goose winning" hung sing motto. Hence, the belief that there are two hung sing choy li fut schools.

The bak sing branch of choy li fut can be traced back to Jeong Yim. Jeong Yim had three principal students. One of them was

9

Louie Chun, who had a student named Tam Sam. Tam Sam had a choy li fut school in Kwangchow, in a district called Siu Bak (which translates as "little north"). His school bore the name Siu Bak Hung Sing Choy Li Fut Club. That name was too long to be spoken comfortably, so it was changed to Bak Sing Choy Li Fut. To pay respects to their teacher, Tam Sam's students referred to themselves as the bak sing branch of choy li fut.

In 1979, in Hong Kong, all of the choy li fut schools agreed to unite as one system under the name choy li fut. The names hung sing and bak sing are used only to identify the origins of the particular branch.

The Green Grass Monk Misconception

One popular story among some choy li fut historians is that Jeong Yim (sometimes known as Jeong Hung Sing) was one of choy li fut's original founders. This misconception came about from a popular novel of Southern China called *Fut San Hung Sing Kwoon (Hung Sing Studio in Fut San)* by Nim Fut San Yen.

Fut San Hung Sing Kwoon is a fictional story which portrays Jeong Yim's life from his childhood, when he studied kung-fu from Chan Heung in a village called Chan Village, to his career as a kung-fu teacher in Fut San. According to the novel, Chan Heung was allowed to teach only Chan villagers in Chan Village. But after Chan Heung became involved in a fight over water rights and was severely injured, young Jeong Yim emerged from the crowd of bystanders, and with his small amount of kung-fu saved Chan Heung.

To reward the boy for saving his life, Chan Heung vowed to teach Jeong Yim, even though he wasn't from the Chan Village. Jeong Yim stayed in Chan Heung's school as a servant and secretly learned kung-fu at night. He became very proficient at it over the years, and no one in Chan Village knew the carefully guarded secret.

Much later, during a festive lion dance at the Chan Village temple to celebrate Kwan Kung's birthday, many of the villagers were consuming large amounts of rice wine and showing off their kung-fu sets. Jeong Yim, equally as tipsy on rice wine, showed them some of Chan Heung's choy li fut forms, and the secret was out.

As soon as the village elders discovered Jeong Yim's secret, they decided to expel him from Chan Village. Before he left, Jeong Yim met Chan Heung secretly one night. His teacher gave him money and a letter of recommendation to a famous Shaolin temple survivor known as the "green grass monk" who lived at Bot Pai mountain in Kwangsi province.

Jeong Yim found the monk, whose name was Ching Cho. Ching Cho ("green grass" monk) was an expert in fut gar, Buddhist-style kung-fu, which he had learned at the Shaolin temple. After many years of study with the green grass monk, Jeong Yim was given the name "Hung Sing" by Ching Cho. Hung Sing translates as "Hung Party winning." Ching Cho also appointed Jeong Yim to recruit people for the revolution to fight against the Manchurian outsiders.

Jeong Yim left the monk soon after and returned to the Chan village to find Chan Heung and work with him to promote the revolution. Jeong Yim taught Chan Heung everything that he had learned from the green grass monk, and together they completed the choy li fut system.

They made up eight original forms or sets to provide training in all aspects of choy li fut. These forms were called "tai," "ping," "tien," "gwok," "cheung," "on," "mon," and "nin." The eight forms represented the Tai Ping Tien Gwok Kingdom—"peaceful Heavenly kingdom for ten thousand years" that ruled China for two decades.

After that, Jeong Yim traveled to Fut San to establish his own choy li fut hung sing school, while Chan Heung stayed in Chan Village to continue with his revolutionary work.

That is the story propagated by Nim Fut San Yen's book, a story mistakenly believed by many martial artists. By carefully examining the novel, it's easy to spot many errors of fact.

1) The Chan Village of the novel didn't exist. However, Chan Heung's hometown of King Mui did. The dates and years of Chan Heung's stay in King Mui are actually recorded there.

2) It is hard to picture a martial artist of Chan Heung's repu- tation getting hurt in a fight over water rights and being saved by a child who knew a little kung-fu.

3) The statement that Chan Heung's village did not allow outsiders to be taught kung-fu is questionable. One of Chan Heung's first eighteen disciples was an outsider, Lung Ji Choi. Lung Ji Choi was at least twenty to thirty years older than Jeong Yim.

4) There is no historical evidence that the "green grass monk" ever existed.

5) The story that the monk gave Jeong Yim the name "Hung Sing" isn't plausible. At that time, according to available records, Chan Heung was already using that slogan in King Mui.

6) Even today, it isn't accepted for a student to teach his sifu any outside techniques. The China of the late 1800s was even more close-minded. How could Jeong Yim have taught kung-fu to his sifu?

7) Only *"ping* kuen" and "tit jin *cheong* kuen" actually exist in the choy li fut system as original sets. Any of the other supposedly original eight forms were recently made up by people who read the book.

8) Jeong Yim didn't found hung sing choy li fut in Fut San. Chan Din Yao and Chan Din Fune founded the fut san choy li fut school in 1848. Jeong Yim came later and reopened the school.

With the absence of verifiable historical records, it is hard to consider the "green grass monk" story as fact—or even as a reasonable possibility.

The Choy Li Fut Altar

It is traditional within the choy li fut system that every legitimate school have an altar honoring the system and its past masters. In 1848, when the original eighteen disciples branched out beyond King Mui, Chan Heung wrote a couplet that all choy li fut schools could use to identify themselves.

The dictionary defines "couplet" as "two successive lines of verse, usually rhyming and in the same meter, that form a unit," and that describes Chan Heung's couplet perfectly. Printed in black Chinese characters on a red background, the two halves of the couplet frame pictures of Chan Heung and the late grand masters (past masters). The first character of each side

The Choy Li Fut couplet

Hero

雄	Strong	Graceful	英
拳	Fist	Staff	棍
放	Release	Fly	飛
出	Out	Above	騰
虎	Tiger	Dragon	龍
昂	Raise	Wiggle	擺
頭	Head	Tail	尾

can be combined together to make the word "hero" *(ying-hung)*. The left side reads "ying guen fei tun lung bai mei" or "graceful staff flying above dragon wiggling tail." The right side of the couplet reads "hung kuen fong chut fu ong tao" or "strong fist release out tiger raises head." When read top to bottom in the Chinese manner, similar words line up opposite one another.

Since in ancient China anything red had the power of fire to scare off evil creatures, the couplet is printed on a red background. In the past, General Kwan Kung's picture, or a plaque with the past masters' names was always placed in the center, between the two couplet halves. However, in present times, the custom is to display photographs of choy li fut's founder, Chan Heung, and of departed grand masters.

This practice gives appropriate recognition to those who have handed down the art through the ages. It also provides a reminder to the choy li fut student that Chan Heung, who could easily have named his system after himself as did many other kung-fu founders, wanted to recognize the efforts of his own teachers by naming his system after them.

On either side of Chan Heung's picture is his own couplet, "choy li fut moon yuen chi-jo Sil Lum jung pai duck jen chuin," or "I am choy li fut's original founder, but the art was passed down to me from the Shaolin temple."

Students place incense, flowers, and fruit on the choy li fut altar to entice friendly spirits to stay in the kung-fu studio. Fruit is offered to appease any hungry spirits that might enter the school.

Choy li fut students are expected to salute the photographs of the past masters both when entering and leaving the school. This isn't done as a gesture of worship, but rather to give credit and respect to them for their teaching and philosophy. The past masters were all great teachers and choy li fut sifus hope that the serious student will remember them as examples in his kung-fu training.

The First Stage of Training

Body structure (whether the student is strong or weak, old or young, male or female) and mental ability are determining factors when choosing the right kung-fu system to study.

If the system's forms aren't suited to the student's learning ability, there is no benefit to learning them, and the student's health could be ruined. Some kung-fu styles fashion their forms training around techniques that only certain individuals can master.

When Chan Heung designed choy li fut's first training forms, he wanted to fit them to the average student's ability. This gives most people the ability to learn choy li fut thoroughly and master many of its techniques.

There are two stages of training in the choy li fut system, and each primary stage is divided into three levels.

The first basic training level of choy li fut, in which the student learns the primary forms or sets of the choy li fut system, sets the pattern for the student's martial arts future.

However, before learning any forms, students practice stance training. There are two types of stance training in the choy li fut system: high stances (go jong mah) and low stances (dai jong mah). Beginning students always start with the open and wide low stances which strengthen the student's legs and give him a good foundation. These low stances are not too low and wide, or the student wouldn't be able to move quickly and smoothly and his footwork would become stiff and slow, instead of lively and flowing.

When the beginner advances to the high stance, his footwork becomes quicker and the distance covered is shorter. High stances are good for the quick movements required in combat, but they don't have the balance and stability inherent in the lower stances.

Forms training in the choy li fut system is designed to promote health and longevity first and to provide self-defense training second. The practice of choy li fut sets develops the student's muscles and bones, thereby conditioning the body evenly. Every

movement is natural, whether it is hand techniques, footwork, or breathing exercises. No movements in the forms are tense or stiff, which would be detrimental to the student's health.

All choy li fut forms begin with long, wide open circular movements. These techniques are natural and contain no tense force. One advantage to long-arm, open, circular forms is that the *ging* ("power") flows without disturbing the student's continuity and balance. He learns to relax all physical aspects of his body (bone and muscle), his breathing becomes deeper and his energy sinks down to the *tan tien* area (said to be the body's center of internal energy).

While studying the basic stance training forms, the choy li fut student learns to produce vocal sounds that match his movements and help him to produce ging. The five sounds, "yak," "wak," "dik," "hay," and "ha," force the student to produce the appropriate ging by changing his breathing patterns.

The choy li fut student learns to pay attention to his breathing techniques when practicing the forms. First of all, he has to breathe regularly. This makes him more active and gives him more power. When he strikes out and releases power, he exhales. When he pulls back, he inhales. When he sinks down in a stance, he exhales. When he rises up, he inhales. When he "closes the door" to block an oncoming attack, he exhales. When he "opens his door" to launch an attack, he inhales.

Because these breathing exercises are not natural to the beginning student, he's taught to take a break and rest if he overdoes a movement and exhausts himself. The use of ging by a tired and unconditioned person can cause internal damage. With time and practice, all of the power-releasing exercises become natural.

In order to keep his form and posture accurate and correct, the beginning student is not allowed to progress too quickly. If he is in too much of a hurry to improve, his breathing won't match his movements and he could damage his circulation, joints, and muscles.

By conditioning and relaxing his body with long circular movements and by producing sounds that help regulate the type of power put forth, the choy li fut practitioner is training in both external and internal aspects at the same time, bringing them together as one function.

Chan Heung set down ten important training principles for the student to follow to be successful in choy li fut:

1) He must have an experienced teacher.
2) He must work hard.
3) If he has to use his martial knowledge in combat, he should focus all of his intent to win the battle.
4) He should conserve sexual activities to preserve his chi.
5) He must have good nutrition.
6) When he strikes, he must release great power.
7) is stamina must be good.
8) He must breathe properly.
9) When defending himself, he should never give the opponent an opening or opportunity.
10) He must take the time to be stable and balanced in his footwork. His footwork is the foundation of choy li fut.

The first form learned in choy li fut is called *ng lun ma* ("five wheel stance"). This set includes all of the basic footwork and stances, both high and low.

After ng lun ma, the choy li fut student learns *ng lun chui* ("five wheel fist"). All of the basic fists and hand techniques are combined with the basic footwork in this form.

These two basic forms can be compared to the construction of a tall building. The form is like the foundation, set deep into the ground. With a strong solid foundation, the building can withstand any storm.

Students should always remember that the choy li fut basics are like the foundation of a sturdy skyscraper. They should not be in a hurry to learn more and more forms. If they are, their sets may be attractive and pretty to watch, but they won't be practical.

When learning and practicing footwork and hand techniques, the choy li fut student should be aware that "all small and tight starts from big and wide; all tall starts from low; all tight starts from loose." In other words, by practicing long circular hand techniques, it's easier to learn the short. By practicing wide low stances, it's easier to learn high stances. And by learning to be loose and relaxed, it's easier to develop strong power.

Footwork

All of the basic footwork and hand techniques of choy li fut are contained within the two foundation forms, *ng lun ma* ("five-wheel stance") and *ng lun chui* ("five-wheel fist").

There are many benefits of learning the five-wheel stance set. Not only do students develop strength in their legs, and balance in their stances, but they also learn a form of moving meditation, which is the beginning stage of chi development.

The foundation stances that are found in the five-wheel stance are:

1) **Sei ping ma.** This stance is sometimes called a "square horse position." The student stands in a low position with both legs equidistant from his body. His toes always point forward, and his knees turn out slightly. Sei ping ma is a stable, secure stance, which is good for strengthening the student's legs and providing a solid foundation. If the choy li fut student is moving and looking to the left, the stance is called left sei ping ma. If he's moving to the right, it is a right sei ping ma. When the student looks to the front, it's a front sei ping ma.

2) **Diu ma.** Known as a cat stance in other martial arts, this stance puts 20 percent of the student's weight on his front foot and 80 percent on the back leg. Diu ma is useful when waiting for an offensive movement from the opponent. The choy li fut practitioner can move from this stance easily in either direction and still maintain his balance and readiness. If the right foot is forward, it is a right diu ma. When the left foot is forward, it becomes a left diu ma.

3) **Nau ma.** Sometimes called "twist horse," this solid stance is formed by turning the front leg 90 degrees and bending the knee. This causes the student to drop into a low stance with 80 percent of his weight on his front leg. Only the toe of his rear foot touches the floor. Nau ma requires a lot of waist action, and gives the student more length to his reach because his waist is turned to extend his front hand further. His back foot can easily be converted into a kicking or advancing foot. Nau ma is versatile, changing quickly into any of choy li fut's other stances.

4) **Tau ma.** Tau ma is similar to nau ma, except that it is always a retreating stance. To form tau ma, the practitioner places his front leg behind his rear leg, causing him to retreat slightly. Tau ma can be translated as "stealing horse."

5) **Ding-ji ma.** Sometimes known as *ji ng ma* or "wedge stance," ding-ji ma is similar to the bow-and-arrow stances of other martial arts systems. The purpose of the ding-ji ma stance is to provide the choy li fut stylist with a stronger base or foundation for more extension and force. The student's weight is placed evenly between the front and rear legs. His rear heel is pushed outwards to provide even more stability. Ding-ji ma can be formed with either the right or left foot forward.

6) **Lok quei ma.** Called "kneeling horse" because it requires an almost kneeling position, lok quei ma provides a stable base from which to attack low areas of the opponent's body. The practitioner's front foot is firmly planted, bearing 70 percent of his weight. Only the toe of his rear foot is in contact with the ground. The student's back knee should be turned outward to provide more stability. If his right knee is down, it is a right kneeling horse. If his left knee is down, the stance is called left kneeling horse.

7) **Duk lup ma.** Other styles call this a "crane stance." It is a one-legged position used to block an oncoming kick. In the choy li fut system, if the right leg is raised, it's called *don hei yao gu ek*. When the left leg is up, it becomes *don hei jor gu ek*. Although it is a one-legged stance, duk lup ma is stable enough to be used in conjunction with hand techniques.

Other commonly seen stances in the choy li fut system are:
1) **Sieh ma.** This is the reverse of ding-ji ma. It is a low slanted horse stance, and is more defensive than ding-ji ma.

2) **Quai ma.** Called "cross horse," this is the forward moving version of tau ma ("stealing horse"). It is the opposite of stealing horse, in that the student's back foot crosses in front of his front foot, causing him to move slightly forward. This stance allows the stylist to move forward quickly and still maintain his stability. It can be easily converted into other stances.

3) **Sow geuk.** This is a sweep. Sweeps are an important part of choy li fut. The student's waist creates the maximum power necessary to bring down an opponent.

4) **Da seung fei.** Called a "turning butterfly kick," it lets the practitioner kick both low and high to an opponent behind him. The student will actually reverse directions in the air while kicking.

The student also learns how to advance and retreat while practicing the five-wheel stance set. This is important for maintaining balance and strategic position in combat.

The one kick seen in five-wheel stance is a straight thrust kick, coming from the practitioner's side, rather than his front, in order to provide the smallest target possible to an opponent. In kung-fu language, this is "keeping the door closed to attack."

Other kicks common to choy li fut are:

1) **Tsang geuk.** This is a side kick, striking with the side of the foot.

2) **Ding geuk.** Ding geuk is an inside crescent kick to the opponent's head or neck.

3) **Kwa tui.** The opposite of ding geuk, kwa tui is an outside crescent kick.

Fists

Every set in the choy li fut system begins with movements called *hoi jong* ("opening hands"). Hoi jong movements were originated as secret identification signals between choy li fut revolutionaries during the rebellious period of the Ching Dynasty.

Although there are many types of hoi jong movements, each having its own meaning, three of the most popular are vertical, horizontal, and stationary hoi jong. Vertical hoi jong is characterized by footwork forward and to the rear only. The horizontal form moves not only forward but also to the side in an L-shaped pattern. The stationary style remains in one position and uses hand movements only. The hoi jong pattern of five-wheel stance and five-wheel fist is the stationary form.

The choy li fut system contains five variations of fists, each drawn from one of the style's several sources.

The most popular type of fist technique looks like what other styles call a leopard punch. The practitioner's fingers are extended level with his hand to the first knuckle and then folded back into a fist. His thumb lies alongside the index finger to add support. This fist originated from the monk Choy Fok.

The second fist is handed down from Li Yau-San. It is a regular closed fist with the thumb positioned next to the index finger.

Third is the regular closed fist with the thumb lying at a right angle across the fingers. This was the fist originally used in the Shaolin temple, and comes from Chan Yuen Woo.

The fourth fist was Chan Heung's special fist. It looks like Choy Fok's leopard fist except that the thumb is kept below the folded fingers to add even more support. This fist is seen in choy li fut's elephant form.

The fifth and final fist variation is what kung-fu styles call a phoenix eye fist. Here the middle finger of a regular closed fist is supported and pushed forward by the practitioner's thumb, which lies at a right angle across the other fingers. The striking portion of this fist is the second knuckle of the stylist's middle finger.

Since the target area is very small, the student can deliver a much greater force than he could with a regular fist. The phoenix eye fist requires lengthy conditioning of the hand and wrist. It's seen in choy li fut's drunken form, an advanced training set.

Choy li fut's basic fists or hand techniques are all found in five-wheel fist *(ng lun chui)*. They are:

1) **Tsop chui.** This is a straight-forward thrusting punch. It's formed by making a flat fist with the first knuckles of the hand extended and the fingers folded back on themselves. The student's thumb lies flat against the side of his hand and acts as a brace to provide extra strength. With this fist, the practitioner can deliver more force to a smaller target.

Tsop chui comes in several variations. *Yeung tsop* is a straight punch. *Yum tsop* or *loi yum chui* is a tsop chui delivered with a twist of the forearm to gain more power. Yum tsop is like a corkscrew, and is directed at the opponent's groin or ribs.

Cheong ngan chui can be either a straight tsop or a corkscrew-like tsop. It is aimed at the opponent's eyes and can be devastating.

The last tsop chui is called *ping tsop* or *jin chui* ("arrow fist"). It's a flat tsop, made with the back of the hand facing up, instead of sideways as with the other tsops.

Leopard Punch

Li Yall-San's Punch

Chan Yuen Woo's Punch

Chan Heung's Special Fist

28

Pheonix Eye Fist

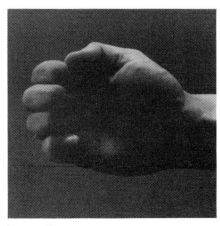

Yueng Tsop

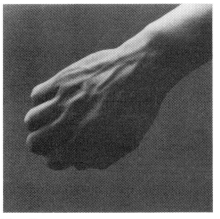

Yum Tsop

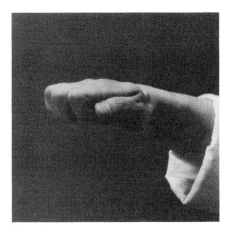

Ping Tsop

2) **Kwa chui.** This is a backfist or vertical back strike. In choy li fut, backfists are performed with very definite circular motions. Even short-hand kwa chuis contain a noticeable circular pattern. This allows the stylist to pick up extra momentum and to use the maximum benefit of his waist action. Kwa chui is also seen in a horizontal form called dot chui or bin chui.

3) **Jong.** Jong is a powerful uppercut, also called pow chui. The action used to form jong is an upward circle which uses the whole body for power. Power starts at the feet and works its way through the body in a big circle, until it exits from the fist.

4) **Sow chui.** This is the knockout punch of choy li fut. It's a roundhouse which is delivered with all the power of the practitioner's waist. A well-delivered sow chui has an arc of over 200 degrees. The striking area can be either the side of the fist, the back of the fist with the arm turned inward, or the front of the fist. In five-wheel fist, the striking portion is the side of the fist.

An upper sow chui is called *lam chui*. A horizontal sow chui, aimed at the opponent's kidneys, is named *wang sow chui*. A sow chui traveling vertically downward is called *kei sow chui*.

5) **Pek chui.** This is a vertical hammerfist aimed straight down on the opponent's head, neck, or back. A variation of pek chui is called *chin-ji pek chui*. Chin-ji pek chui is a short diagonal blow downwards, striking with the area between the fist and first half of the forearm.

6) **Biu jong.** Biu jong is a horizontal forearm strike aimed at the opponent's chest. It is often used in conjunction with a short sweep to take the opponent down quickly.

7) **Kup chui.** Sometimes called a "stamping fist," it is just that. Kup chui comes straight down in an overhead circular pattern. Contact is made with the front of the fist—specifically, the first knuckles of the fingers.

8) **Jit fu chui.** Translated as "blocking tiger fist," this is similar to a chin-ji pek chui, except that jit fu chui is delivered in an outward direction to block a sweep or low kick.

9) **Lau kiu.** Lau kiu is sometimes called the "scooping fist." It's used to block a center kick.

Choy li fut's palm strikes originate its Shaolin temple background. The most important open-hand strikes are:

1) **Chuin nau.** Also called "anchor hand," chuin nau is effective for blocking an oncoming punch and then immediately grabbing the attacker with the chuin nau hand. It can also be used to touch and grab. Chuin nau is an outward and sideways palm.

2) **Lok kiu.** Referred to in choy li fut as a "grinding wheel grab," lok kiu is a two-hand grab and pull downwards of the opponent's arm and wrist.

3) **Teut jeung.** Translated as "spread palm," this is a thrust into the opponent's throat region with the front palm, while the back hand helps maintain balance.

4) **Poon kiu.** This is an inward and downward circular block.

5) **Dip jeung.** Known as "butterfly palm," this is a method of locking the opponent's arm or elbow by trapping it close to the student's own body with both hands.

6) **Gong jeung.** Gong jeung is an uppercut palm thrust made to the opponent's jaw.

7) **Don lon.** This is a single-palm horizontal strike to the opponent's solar plexus. The striking area is from the palm to the middle of the forearm.

8) **Twei jeung.** Twei jeung is a two-hand palm push used to push the opponent off balance.

9) **Yeung kiu.** Also called "mirror hand" because it looks like the practitioner is holding a hand mirror, yeung kiu is an outward block.

10) **Kum sau.** This is called "covering palm" and is a palm strike straight down to block a kick or break a wrist grab.

11) **Fu jao.** Fu jao or "tiger claw" is one of the most effective and powerful palm strikes in the choy li fut system. The fingers are formed into a claw hand that is used to grab and tear downward at the opponent's face and eyes.

Weapons

Since Chan Heung's teachers were from both Northern and Southern China, the choy li fut system contains almost all of kung-fu's weapons. Major Southern weapons include the staff, the broadsword, butterfly knives, and double broadswords. Northern China is represented by the spear, the double-edged sword, the double-hook swords, and the three-section staff.

Due to its strong Southern influence, choy li fut has incorporated practical weapons, such as the twin axes, the farmer's hoe, the fan, and the horse bench, into its retinue of weapons.

Traditional Chinese weapons, heavy with history, are also to be found in choy li fut. These include the kwan-do (General Kwan's knife), trident, monk's shovel, and Chinese daggers.

All choy li fut weapons hold a place in the serious student's training schedule. Staff training, for instance, is a form of weight training that conditions the student's forearms. Training with the delicate double-edged sword promotes stronger and more flexible wrist action.

Double weapons such as the butterfly knives and double broad swords add an equal amount of weight to each hand, giving the student more extension and improving his balance. Double weapons teach the student to use both hands instead of relying on just one.

Even though this is an age of firearms, the knowledge obtained from studying traditional Chinese weapons can still be useful. If accosted, the student can pick up a long stick or even a broom handle and use it like a staff. Or he can grab a short stick and effectively apply broadsword techniques with it.

It's also fun to practice with equipment instead of just bare hands. Weapons training is always a good challenge, since the weapons techniques differ greatly from one another.

Although the kwan-do is a useless weapon for modern self-defense, when the student imitates General Kwan Kung stroking his beard and riding his horse in the kwan-do set, he is building his own spirit and sense of value. Weapons training gives the student more understanding of China's culture and history, an important facet of martial arts.

Staff

Kwan-do

Two-Man Forms

Choy li fut's two-man forms are an important part of the advanced student's training. Two-man sets, which include both empty hands and weapons forms, help the student develop his timing, focus, and distance. They teach him correct applications and let him practice against someone else. Because there is contact involved, the practitioner conditions and strengthens his forearms.

Choy li fut is different from many other kung-fu systems in that other styles teach their students individual and continuous self-defense techniques, which are sometimes hard to remember. The choy li fut system puts all of its self-defense techniques into structured patterns involving two people. There are many such forms at each level of training in choy li fut. They include empty hand sets, weapons sets (such as spear versus sword, staff against staff, and three-section staff versus spear), and empty hands versus weapons (empty hands against the double daggers).

After the student masters the two-man forms, his reactions in combat will be second nature.

Two-man sets lead into free-style sparring. No kung-fu is practical without this type of training, and two-man forms provide a good transition from individual forms practice to the actual contact needed for sparring.

Training Aids

One of the more important mechanical training aids in the choy li fut system is the wall bag set. Although it is not a traditional form, it includes the practical application of all the basic hands and footwork that the student learned in five-wheel fist and five-wheel stance.

The purpose of the wall bag form is to develop and condition the student's palms and fists by giving him a solid, unyielding target preferable to the hanging bag that moves away when struck. The student has the opportunity to practice his power on a target that he can't injure.

The wall bag set is different from the sets of other kung-fu systems, most of which have the student stay in one position and punch the bag. The choy li fut set has a great deal of variety in footwork and direction of attack.

The set consists of 50 movements, all of which are offensive. It should be practiced a minimum of five times per day for several years. After that, the student will have conditioned his hands and mastered the techniques in the form.

When training on the wall bag, the student should hit the bag hard enough to feel it, but not hard enough to hurt himself. He shouldn't try to punch through it, because it won't move. If he hits it too hard, he can ruin his knuckles, injure other joints, and damage himself internally. He shouldn't fully extend his elbow when he strikes the bag, or he can injure the sensitive elbow joint. Every student needs a good instructor to demonstrate the proper way to attack the wall bag.

1) Feet together, fists on hips.

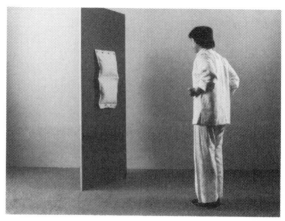

2) Left foot crosses right to right sei ping ma, right kwa chui to upper bag, left hand behind.

3) Right ding-ji ma, left tsang-jeung to lower bag, right fist behind.

4) Turn to right sei ping ma, right tsop to lower bag, left hand protects at elbow.

5) Right nau ma, left tsang jeung, lower bag, right fist behind.

6) Forward left diagonal ding-ji ma, right chin-ji to upper bag, left hand protects at elbow.

7) Left tau ma, left yum tsop to lower bag, right fist behind.

8) Turn to right sei ping ma, right fan jong to upper bag, left hand protects head.

9) Forward right diagonal ding-ji ma, left kup chui to upper bag, right hand behind.

10) Left foot retreats half step back to right sei ping ma, right don-lon to lower bag, left hand protects at elbow.

11) Right ding-ji ma, left fu jao to upper bag, right hand protects at elbow.

12) Right foot crosses to west, right yum-wat to lower bag, left hand protects at elbow.

13) Turn to left sei ping ma, left kwa chui to upper bag, right hand behind.

14) Left ding-ji ma, right kup chui to upper bag, left hand behind.

15) Turn to left sei ping ma, left fan jong to upper bag, right hand protects head.

60

16) Left nau ma, right tsang-jeung to lower bag, left fist behind.

17) Forward right diagonal ding-ji ma, left chin-ji to upper bag, right hand protects at elbow.

18) Right tau ma, right yum tsop to lower bag, left hand behind.

19) Turn to left sei ping ma, left gong jeung to upper bag, right hand protects head.

20) Forward left diagonal ding-ji ma, right kup chui to upper bag, left hand behind.

21) Right foot steps back half step to left sei ping ma, left dot chui to lower bag, right hand protects at elbow.

22) Left ding-ji ma, right gong jeung to upper bag, left hand protects at elbow.

23) Cross left foot to west, left kwa chui to upper bag, right hand protects at elbow.

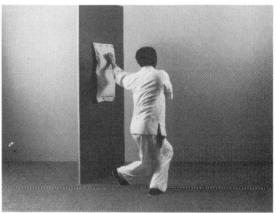

24) Left quai ma, left yum-wat to lower bag, right-hand protects at elbow.

25) Left foot retreats to south, right sei ping ma, right dot chui to lower bag, left hand protects elbow.

26) Left foot steps horizontally forward to right diu ma, right cheong ngan chui to upper bag, left hand protects at elbow.

27) Right diu ma, left chuin nau to upper bag, right hand at elbow.

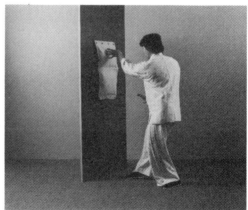

28) Right diu ma, right tsop chui to lower bag, left hand protects at elbow.

29) Left foot steps forward to NE, right foot retreats half step to left sei ping ma, left biu jong to upper bag, right hand protects at elbow.

30) Right foot steps forward to west, turn to left ding-ji ma, right yum tsop to lower bag, left fist behind.

31) Left sei ping ma, left tsop chui to lower bag, right fist behind.

32) Left nau ma, right kup chui to upper bag, left hand behind.

33) Right quai ma to west, right kwa chui to upper bag, left hand protects at elbow.

66

34) Turn to left sei ping ma, left kwa chui to upper bag, right hand behind.

35) Left foot retreats to horizontal ding-ji ma, right tsop chui to lower bag, left hand behind.

36) Shift right horizontal ding-ji ma to south, left tsop chui to lower bag, right hand behind.

37) Left horizontal diu ma, right kwa chui to upper bag, left hand behind.

38) Right horizontal diu ma, left kwa chui to upper bag, right hand behind.

39) Right foot retreats to horizontal left ding-ji ma, right horizontal sow chui to lower bag, left hand protects at elbow.

40) Left sei ping ma, left don lon to upper bag, right hand behind.

41) Left horizontal ding-ji ma, right sow chui to upper bag, left hand protects at elbow.

42) Pick up left foot, shift forward to left ding-ji ma, double twei jeung (fingers pointing to right) to upper bag.

43) Jump up and switch to left lok quei ma, double twei jeung (fingers pointing to left) to lower bag.

44) Right foot retreats to right horizontal ding-ji ma, left tsang jeung to lower bag, right hand behind.

45) Right horizontal lok quei ma, right tsop chui to lower bag, left hand protects head.

46) Left horizontal lok quei ma, left tsop chui to lower bag, right hand protects head.

47) Left horizontal ding-ji ma, right kwa chui to upper bag, left hand behind.

48) Right horizontal ding-ji ma, left kwa chui to upper bag, right hand behind.

49) Left forward ding-ji ma, double foong jeung to lower bag.

50) Left foot steps back, right foot closes to left, roll fists back to waist and nod.

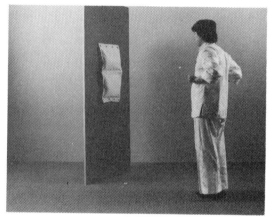

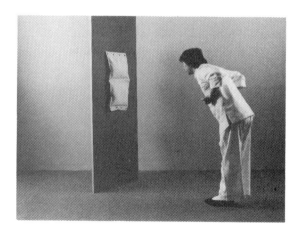

Application to **6**

Application to **9**

Application to **11**

Application to **12**

Application to **17**

Application to **18**

Application to **25**

Application to **26**

Application to **33**

The Chinese term for wooden dummy is *jong*. It is considered necessary foundation training for the serious kung-fu student.

In the choy li fut system, wooden dummy training originated in King Mui village where trees could be easily converted into wooden dummies. Chan Heung taught his wooden dummy techniques only to his sons and his immediate students. His son, Chan Koon Pak, took the dummy training with him to Kwang-chow and passed it on to his own students. Outside of King Mui, only Chan Koon Pak's students knew of choy li fut's wooden dummies. For that reason, not all choy li fut schools teach traditional wooden dummy techniques.

The most popular choy li fut dummy is called the *ching jong* dummy. Ching jong means "balance scale," like the hand-held weight scale used in Chinese herb shops to measure and weigh herbs.

The ching jong dummy has a large wooden arm in the upper middle portion of the dummy. This arm has a short section protruding from the rear of the dummy. From this short section in back was hung a heavy metal weight. The weight allowed the practitioner to pull down and push up on the front part of the upper arm. In present times, a strong metal spring serves the same purpose. From this balanced upper arm the name *ching* ("balance") is derived.

There are two arms in the middle section of the ching jong, and one leg that angles out and down at the lower section of the dummy.

At first glance, the ching jong dummy looks similar to most other wooden dummies. However, other dummies have two small upper arms and one large midsection arm, while the ching jong dummy has one large upper arm and two smaller middle appendages. Also, other dummies' upper arms do not move, as does the ching jong's arm. The choy li fut dummy is created from a log that has been given square corners, while most other dummies are made from round logs.

Ching jong dummies have seven flat sand bags attached to them. There is one bag on the upper portion, one in the center, one on the lower front portion, one each on the upper right and left sides, and one bag on the center right and left sides, for a total of seven bags. The bags are used to practice form and power while striking.

Another popular choy li fut wooden dummy is called *dan wong jong* ("spring dummy"). This device is a solid round log mounted on a large heavy spring. When wrapped with foam padding, this dummy can be used for kicking and punching practice. When hit, the dummy springs away from and then back towards the student. The spring dummy was originally developed to be used outdoors where there was no ceiling from which to hang large sand bags.

The *bot kwa jong* is a dummy used for both hand forms and staff training. It has sand bags or metal plates hanging from its protrusions, which are used either for empty hand blocking and striking or for blocking and poking with a staff.

The choy li fut system also has some specialty dummies that are used with the broadsword, butterfly knives, staff, and even the fan. The dummy used for fan techniques is named *tung yen jong* ("copper man dummy"). It is an acupuncture dummy containing twelve key pressure points for fan and empty hand strikes.

There are 94 movements in the ching jong set, which is an original form passed down from choy li fut's founder.

Dummy training is essential to kung-fu training for several reasons. First, the student can use full power and contact on the wooden dummy, something he can't do while sparring, because no partner wants to receive that much pain. Second, the dummy helps the student learn to judge his distance and focus on the striking area. Since the dummy can't fight back, it won't help the student's timing, but the wooden dummy will provide solid resistance to the student's blows.

Finally, the dummy will condition the student's arms, wrists, shins, fingers, palms, fists, legs, and feet. The ching jong sand bags condition the student's fists and claw hands, and the dummy's arms toughen the practitioner's arms and palms for blocking. Shins and feet are conditioned by sweeping and kicking the dummy's leg.

Although the wooden dummy is stationary, the footwork used includes all of the stances and movements of choy li fut. Since there are sand bags placed all around the dummy, the student can move in three directions and practice every type of footwork.

Second-Stage Training

The second level of training in the choy li fut system combines soft and hard and is called *chui hop gong yao.*

Chui is translated as "up and down follow each other together." This means that the waist and legs work in conjunction.

Both waist and legs must be flexible. The student gets this flexibility by working hard at the horse stance and basic forms training, until he has learned to coordinate his hands and footwork and has built a solid foundation.

The waist is the most important part of the martial artist's body. When he changes direction, his waist controls the movement and his body follows. When the student releases power, he uses his waist and back together. According to a famous kung-fu proverb, "Any kind of exercise that doesn't use the waist is like a clock with no hands."

Footwork is the base of the choy li fut system. When the stylist releases power through his fist or counters an opponent's attack, his stance has to be stable, heavy, strong, and flexible. Another proverb says, "Before you learn the hands, you have to learn to walk." This means that if the student hasn't mastered the footwork, his hands are useless. When the student's waist and footwork are together and he releases power, he'll have control.

Hop refers to the combination of internal and external powers. Internal energy includes strength derived from the practitioner's *chi,* spirit, and libido. External power, on the other hand, is the energy of the body, hands, and feet.

Gong yao, literally translated, means "hard and soft helping each other to produce *ging.* Ging is the Chinese word for the power that is produced from an interaction of internal (soft) and external (hard) energies.

Ging is necessary in any phase of fighting. According to Chan Heung's original writing, "No matter whether you're attacking or dissolving, you have to use ging. If you don't, you're not stable and flexible and cannot control the opponent."

Ging is sometimes defined as "wisdom of strength" or "using strength wisely." It takes time to develop, and the student has to work hard, learning to use his muscles and direct his power in a new way.

Before studying ging, the beginning student's muscular power is tense and brutal. He may look strong, but his actual force is limited and he readily burns energy.

When he learns to correctly direct his ging, it will look as if he's not using any muscular strength. But in reality, the ging or power is released from his body like lightning.

There are four primary types of ging in the choy li fut system:

1) **Nim chuin ging**. This is "sticky reeling ging" and means that the kung-fu practitioner is "tied together with his opponent," that is, in physical contact with his adversary without giving him a chance to get away.

Nim chuin ging is the most important form of power. When the student trains to develop this ging, he has to relax his whole body and concentrate on producing feeling and sensitivity. When he accomplishes this, then no matter where the opponent goes, he can follow and control him. He follows his opponent's reaction by feeling. Even though he doesn't initiate the attack, he is still in control. If his opponent doesn't move, the choy li fut practitioner doesn't move. If the opposition moves, even slightly, then the practitioner is the first to move decisively.

2) **Gok ging**. Translated as "enlightened ging," this is the second most important type of power emitted by the choy li fut practitioner. The term "enlightened" means that the student first learns to know himself, then the opponent.

The student must have learned nim chuin ging well before he can master gok ging. He practices being quiet and calm, using soft against hard. It can be compared to the fighting style of a snake, which waits quietly for his prey and strikes hard and fast when it appears. Gok ging is produced from an internal calmness that allows the student to strike with loose relaxed power, instead of with the hard tense power that results from fear and apprehension.

3) **Woi shun ging**. This is a spiraling, rotating power that allows the student to follow his opponent as if he were a boomerang. No matter where the opponent goes, the rounded circling woi shun ging follows, dissolves the attack and creates an opening for a counterattack. This ging is said to "come and go, but also stay in the same spot." The practitioner uses his woi shun ging to redirect his opponent's direction of attack. When he gains control, he releases more ging. Waist action controls this power entirely.

4) **Gum gong ging**. The fourth important power, this ging is translated to mean "hardness," like a diamond. Again, the student must know nim chuin, gok, and woi shun before he can understand this ging, which combines hard and soft to release a strong hard force. However, it's not a *tense* force. The Chinese

say, "Hard carries soft and soft carries hard to produce a balanced complete power."

Gum gong ging brings together the previous three gings to produce the proper timing, control, and direction. The practitioner looks loose and relaxed because he's combined the three previous gings in sequence, with the result being gum gong ging, an unhesitating fast, hard strike which has great impact.

When the student is able to combine the action of his waist and legs with his external and internal energies and with his ging, he will have mastered the second level of choy li fut training.

Ng Lun Ma—
Five-Wheel Stance

1) Attention position—feet together, arms down.

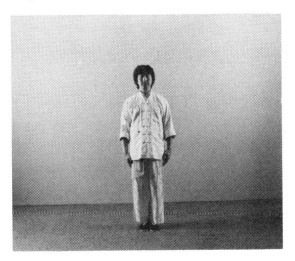

2) Double yeung-kiu.

3) Ding yeut ("palms pressing moon").

4) Double chum kiu ("sword finger") down.

82

5) Double san kiu ("sword finger") up.

6) Gum jin ("golden scissors").

7) Double fun sau (flip palms out and back).

8) Cha you (hands to hips).

9) Open step to sei ping ma (toe-heels two times).

10) Turn shoulders to right.

11) Left foot steps back to right diu ma, right elbow down.

12) Right kick, shift forward to right sei ping ma.

13) Turn shoulders to right.

14) Left foot steps back to right diu ma, right elbow down.

15) Right kick, shift forward to right sei ping ma.

16) Turn shoulders to right.

17) Left foot steps back to right diu ma, right elbow down.

18) Right kick, shift forward to right diu ma.

19) Turn shoulders to right.

20) Turn shoulders to left.

21) Right foot steps back to left diu ma, left elbow down.

22) Left kick, shift forward to left sei ping ma.

23) Turn shoulders to left.

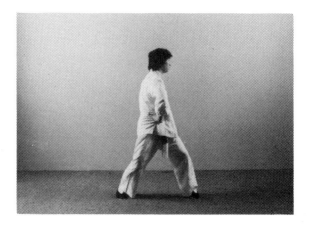

24) Right foot steps back to left diu ma, left elbow down.

25) Left kick, shift forward to left sei ping ma.

26) Turn shoulders to left.

27) Right foot steps back to left diu ma, left elbow down.

28) Left kick, shift forward to left sei ping ma.

29) Turn shoulders to left.

30) Turn shoulders to right.

31) Circle right foot to right nau ma, left elbow down.

32) Left kick, shift forward to left sei ping ma.

33) Turn shoulders to left.

34) Circle left foot to left nau ma, right elbow down.

35) Right kick, shift forward to right sei ping ma.

36) Turn shoulders to right.

37) Circle right foot to right nau ma, left elbow down.

38) Left kick, shift forward to left sei ping ma.

39) Turn shoulders to left.

40) Circle left foot to left nau ma, right elbow down.

41) Right kick, shift forward to right sei ping ma.

42) Turn shoulders to right.

43) Turn shoulders to left.

44) Circle left foot to left nau ma, right elbow down.

45) Right kick, shift forward to right sei ping ma.

46) Turn shoulders to right.

47) Circle right foot to right nau ma, left elbow down.

48) Left kick, shift forward to left sei ping ma.

49) Turn shoulders to left.

50) Circle left foot to left nau ma, right elbow down.

51) Right kick, shift forward to right sei ping ma.

52) Turn shoulders to right.

53) Circle right foot to right nau ma, left elbow down.

54) Left kick, shift forward to left sei ping ma.

55) Turn shoulders to left.

56) Step back left foot to right diu ma, right elbow down.

57) Step back right foot to left diu ma, left elbow down.

58) Step back left foot to right diu ma, right elbow down.

59) Step back right foot to left diu ma, left elbow down.

60) Step back left foot to right diu ma, right elbow down.

61) Step back right foot to left diu ma, left elbow down.

62) Turn to right diu ma.

63) Step back right foot to left diu ma, left elbow down.

64) Step back left foot to right diu ma, right elbow down.

65) Step back right foot to left diu ma, left elbow down.

66) Step back left foot to right diu ma, right elbow down.

67) Step back right foot to left diu ma, left elbow down.

68) Step back left foot to right diu ma, right elbow down.

69) Turn to left diu ma.

70) Turn to right diu ma.

71) Shift right foot forward.

72) Turn to left diu ma.

73) Turn to right diu ma.

74) Shift right foot forward.

75) Turn to left diu ma.

76) Turn to right diu ma.

77) Shift right foot forward.

78) Turn to left diu ma.

79) Shift left foot forward.

80) Turn to right diu ma.

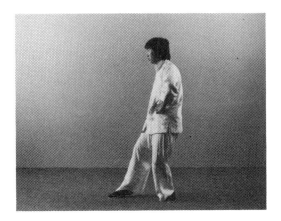

81) Turn to left diu ma.

82) Shift left foot forward.

83) Turn to right diu ma.

84) Turn to left diu ma.

85) Shift left foot forward.

86) Turn to right diu ma.

87) Turn to left diu ma.

88) Shift to left ding-ji ma, shoulder to left.

89) Left lok quei ma, shoulder to right.

90) Right lok quei ma, shoulder to left.

91) Right ding-ji ma forward, shoulder to right.

92) Left foot shifts back, pick up right foot, double chuin-nau.

93) Cross right foot to right quai ma, drop hands toward right hip, right peet jeung.

94) Cross left foot to left quai ma, circle hands overhead to left hip.

95) Shift forward to right sei ping ma, right don-lon.

96) Right foot closes to left foot, double fun sau.

97) Fists roll back to hip (feet together).

98) In same position, nod head.

Ng Lun Chui— Five-Wheel Fist

1) Attention position—feet together, fists on hips.

2) Step out to right, front sei ping ma.

3) Shift right, right sei ping ma, right yum tsop.

4) Left foot steps back to right diu ma, right lau kiu.

5) Shift right, right sei ping ma, right kwa chui.

6) Shift right ding-ji ma, left cheong ngan chui.

7) Shift right, right sei ping ma, right yum tsop.

8) Left foot steps back to right diu ma, right lau kiu.

9) Shift right, right sei ping ma, right kwa chui.

10) Shift right ding-ji ma, left cheong ngan chui.

11) Shift right, right sei ping ma, right yum tsop.

12) Left foot steps back to right diu ma, right lau kiu.

13) Shift right, right sei ping ma, right kwa chui.

14) Shift right ding-ji ma, left cheong ngan chui.

15) Shift right, right sei ping ma, right yum tsop.

16) Turn, shift to left sei ping ma, left yum tsop.

17) Right foot steps back to left diu ma, left lau kiu.

18) Shift left, left sei ping ma, left kwa chui.

19) Shift left ding-ji ma, right cheong ngan chui.

20) Shift left, left sei ping ma, left yum tsop.

21) Step back to left diu ma, left lau kiu.

22) Shift left, left sei ping ma, left kwa chui.

23) Shift left ding-ji ma, right cheong ngan chui.

24) Shift left, left sei ping ma, left yum tsop.

25) Step back to left diu ma, left lau kiu.

124

26) Shift left, left sei ping ma, left kwa chui.

27) Shift left ding-ji ma, right cheong ngan chui.

28) Shift left, left sei ping ma, left yum tsop.

29) Step back left foot to right diu ma, right yum tsop.

30) Step back right foot to left diu ma, left yum tsop.

31) Step back left foot to right diu ma, right yum tsop.

32) Step back right foot to left diu ma, left yum tsop.

33) Turn to right diu ma, right yum tsop.

34) Step back right foot to left diu ma, left yum tsop.

35) Step back left foot to right diu ma, right yum tsop.

36) Step back right foot to left diu ma, left yum tsop.

37) Step back left foot to right diu ma, right yum tsop.

38) Right nau ma, right lok kiu.

39) Step forward to left ding-ji ma, double teut jeung.

40) Left nau ma, left lok kiu.

41) Step forward to right ding-ji ma, double teut jeung.

42) Right nau ma, right lok kiu.

43) Step forward to left ding-ji ma, double teut jeung.

44) Left nau ma, left lok kiu.

45) Step forward to right ding-ji ma, double teut jeung.

46) Turn, left nau ma, left lok kiu.

47) Step forward to right ding-ji ma, double teut jeung.

48) Right nau ma, right lok kiu.

49) Step forward to left ding-ji ma, double teut jeung.

50) Left nau ma, left lok kiu.

51) Step forward to right ding-ji ma, double teut jeung.

52) Right nau ma, right lok kiu.

53) Step forward to left ding-ji ma, double teut jeung.

54) Turn, right diu ma, right yeung kiu.

55) Right diu ma, left chuin nau.

56) Right diu ma, left poon kiu.

57) Shift forward to right sei ping ma, right tsop chui.

58) Turn, left sei ping ma, left poon kiu.

59) Left ding-ji ma, right sow chui.

60) Step forward to right sei ping ma, left poon kiu.

61) Right sei ping ma, right pek chui.

62) Turn, right quai ma, dip jeung.

FRONT VIEW

63) Step forward to left sei ping ma, right gong jeung.

64) Right quai ma, right don lon.

65) Step forward to left ding-ji ma, right fan jong.

66) Left sei ping ma, left kum sau.

68) Double teut jeung, right groin kick.

67) Left ding-ji ma, right fu jao.

69) Replace right foot to left ding-ji ma, right gong jeung.

70) Left tou ma, right biu jong.

71) Turn to left ding-ji ma, left kwa chui.

72) Left ding-ji ma, right kup chui, left fist to rear.

73) Forward right sei ping ma, right biu jong.

74) Retreat to right horizontal ding-ji ma, left poon kiu.

75) Right horizontal lok quei ma, right jit fu chui.

76) Don hei yao geuk, ready position for tuei jeung.

77) Shift forward to left lok quei ma, seung twei jeung (double push palm).

78) Left quai ma, left chuin nau.

79) Shift forward to right ding-ji ma, left poon kiu.

FRONT VIEW

80) Right lok quei ma, right tsop chui.

143

81) Right quai ma, drop both outturned fists to right (double fists).

82) Left quai ma, circle both fists past face (chiu tien won sao).

83) Shift forward to left lok quei ma, double dau fu chui (double uppercut), left knee down.

84) Don hei yao geuk, left poon kiu.

85) Same position, right diagonal chin-ji.

86) Same position, right biu jong.

87) Same position, left chuin nau.

88) Same position, left poon kiu.

89) Same position, right cheong ngan chui.

90) Right quai ma, drop both hands to right peet jeung.

91) Left quai ma, circle hands to left side (chiu tien won sao).

92) Shift forward to right sei ping ma, right dot chui.

93) Feet together, roll fists back to hips.

94) Nod.

Appendix:
List of Choy Li Fut Sets

Hand Forms

Five-Wheel Stance	Ng Lun Ma
Five-Wheel Fist	Ng Lung Chui
Small Cross Pattern Hand Form	Siu Sup Ji Kuen
Great Cross Pattern Hand Form	Daaih Sup Ji Kuen
Small Plum Blossom Hand Form	Siu Mui Fa Kuen
Level Hand Form	Ping Kuen
Level Elbow Hand Form	Ping Jiang Kuen
Cross Pattern of Kau-Da Hand Form	Sup Ji Kau Da Kuen
Cross Pattern of Tiger-Blocking Hand Form	Sup Ji Jit Fu Kuen
Bear Man Pa-Kwa Hand Form	Hung Yen Bot-Gwa Kuen
Heart of Pa-Kwa Hand Form	Bot-Gwa Sum Kuen
Small Pa-Kwa Hand Form	Siu Bot-Gwa Kuen
Fighting the Tiger Pa-Kwa Hand Form	Dau Fu Bot-Gwa Kuen
Yee Jong's Pa-Kwa Hand Form	Yee Jong Bot-Gwa Kuen
Plum Blossom Pa-Kwa Hand Form	Mui Fa Bot-Gwa Kuen
Daht-Ting's Pa-Kwa Hand Form	Daht-Ting Bot-Gwa Kuen
Great Pa-Kwa Hand Form	Daaih Bot-Gwa Kuen
Buddha Palm Hand Form	Fut Jeong Kuen
Iron Arrow Long Fist	Tit Jin Cheong Kuen
Buddha Tames Tiger Hand Form	Law Hon Fook Fu Kuen
White Hair Hand Form	Bak-Mo Kuen
Eighteen Buddhas Changing Tendons Hand Form	Sup Bot Law Hon Yik Gun Kuen
Eight Drunken Immortals Hand Form	Jeui Bot Sin Kuen
Continuous Dual Kicking Form	Yin Yeung Teui Lin Wan
Snake Form	Seh Ying Kuen
Crane Form	Hok Ying Kuen
Leopard Form	Pau Ying Kuen

Dragon Form	Lung Ying Kuen
Tiger Form	Fu Ying Kuen
Monkey Form	Hao Ying Kuen
Dragon and Tiger Forms	Lung Fu Kuen
Five Animals Hand Form	Ng Ying Kuen
Ten Animals Hand Form	Sup Ying Kuen

Two-Man Hand Sets

Cross Pattern vs. Plum Blossom Form	Sup Ji Kuen Duei-Chuck Mui Fa Kuen
Golden Leopard vs. Tiger Form	Gam Pau Kuen Duei-Chuck Fu Ying Kuen
Tiger vs. Crane Form	Fu Ying Kuen Duei-Chuck Hok Ying Kuen
Snake vs. Crane Form	Seh Ying Kuen Duei-Chuck Hok Ying Kuen
Dragon vs. Tiger Form	Lung Ying Kuen Duei-Chuck Fu Ying Kuen
Lion vs. Elephant Form	Si Ying Kuen Duei-Chuck Jeong Ying Kuen

Staff Sets

Bin-Gwai Double-Ended Staff	Bin-Gwai Seung Tau Gwun
Double and Single-Ended Staff	Seung Gup Dahn Gwun
Coiling Dragon Double-Ended Staff	Poon Lung Seung Tau Gwun
Plum Blossom Spear/Staff	Mui Fa Cheung Gwun
Great Flag Single-Ended Staff	Daaih Hung Kei Dahn Tau Gwun
Monkey Staff	Hang Jyeh Pang
Constricting Dragon Single-Ended Staff	Chuin Lung Dahn Tau Gwun
Chiao-Sot Single-Ended Staff	Chiao-Sot Dahn Tau Gwun
Driving Dragon Single-Ended Staff	Chim Lung Dahn Tau Gwun
Star Pattern Plum Blossom Staff	Ng Dim Mui Fa Gwun

Single-Edged Sword Sets

Plum Blossom Single Sword	Mui Fa Dahn Do
Pa-Kwa Single Sword	Bot-Gwa Dahn Do
Taming the Tiger Single Sword	Fook Fu Dahn Do
Horse-Cutting or Ghost-Head Broadsword	Chahn Ma Dahn Do *or* Gwai Tau Do
Small Plum Blossom Double Swords	Siu Mui Fa Seung Do
Cross Pattern Plum Blossom Double Swords	Sup Ji Mui Fa Seung Do
Seven Stars Plum Blossom Double Swords	Chut Sing Mui Fa Seung Do
Pa-Kwa Twin Butterflies Double Swords	Bot-Gwa Wu Dip Seung Do

Spear Sets

Left-Right Thirteen Lunges Spear — Jor Yauh Sup Sam Cheung
Hook Spear — Ngau Lim Cheung
Snake Spear — Seh Mau Cheung
Plum Blossom Spear — Mui Fa Cheung

Miscellaneous Single Weapons

Cross Pattern Plum Blossom Three-Sectional Chain Whip — Sup Ji Mui Fa Sam Jit Bin
Green Dragon Twin-Edged Sword — Ching Lung Dahn Gim
Golden Dragon Twin-Edged Sword — Gum Lung Dahn Gim
Hand Breaking Fan — Seui Sau Sin
Flying Dragon Fan — Fei Lung Sin
Farmer's Hoe — Chor Tau
Horse Bench — Cheung Kiu Dang
Choy Yeung's Long-Handled Broadsword — Choy Yeung Daaih Do
Nine-Ring Long-Handled Broadsword — Gau Wan Daaih Do
Spring and Autumn Dynasty Long-Handled Broadsword — Chun Chau Daaih Do
Lahn-Mun-Jaaih Style Long-Handled Broadsword — Lahn Mun Jaaih Do
Cross Pattern Trident — Sup Ji Daaih Pa
Diamond Trident — Gum Gong Daaih Pa
Long-Handled Gik — Fong Tien Wahk Gik
Golden Bell Style Shovel — Gum Jung Chahn
Quarter Moon Style Shovel — Yuet Ngah Chahn
Golden Coin Style Shovel — Gum Chin Chahn
Three-Section Staff — Sam Jit Gwun
Nine Dragon Trident — Gau Lung Chah

Miscellaneous Two-Part Weapons

Double Daggers — Seung Pei Sau
Double Copper Hammers — Seung Tung Chui
Double Copper Cudgels — Seung Tung Gan
Double Hookaxes — Seung Wu Sau Ngau
Sword and Chain-Whip — Dahn Do Bin
Sword and Tiger's Head Shield — Dahn Do Fu Tau Paih
Sword and Rattan Shield — Dahn Do Tang Paih Dip
Twin Dragon Twin-Edged Swords — Seung Lung Gim
Double Axes — Seung Fu Tau

Combat Weapon Sets

Two-Man Combat Single and Double-Ended Staff — Seung Gup Dahn Gwun Dwei Chuck
Double-Ended Staff vs. Horse Bench — Seung Tau Gwun Dwei Chuck Kiu Dahng

Double and Single-Ended Staff vs. Chau-sot Single-Ended Staff	Seung Gup Dahn Gwun Dwei Chuck Chau-sot Gwun
One-Edge Sword vs. Red Tassel Spear	Dahn Do Dwei Chuck Hung Ying Cheung
Double Swords vs. Red Tassel Spear	Seung Do Dwei Chuck Hung Ying Cheung
Double Swords vs. Horse Bench	Seung Do Dwei Chuck Cheung Kiu Dahng
Three-Section Staff vs. Red Tassel Spear	Sam Jit Gwun Dwei Chuck Hung Ying Cheung
Double Swords vs. Nine-Ringed Long-Handled Sword	Seung Do Dwei Chuck Gau Wan Do
Spear vs. Kwan-Do	Hung Ying Cheung Dwei Chuck Kwan-Do
Empty Hands vs. Double Daggers	Hung Sau Yup Seung Pei Sau
Umbrella vs. Double-Ended Staff	Yu San Dwei Chuck Seung Tau Gwun
Farmer's Hoe vs. Horse Bench	Chor Tau Dwei Chuck Cheung Kiu Dahng
Taming Tiger One-Edge Sword vs. Green Dragon Double-Edged Swords	Fook Fu Dahn Do Dwei Chuck Ching Lung Gim
Monkey Staff vs. Fong Tien Wahk Gik	Hahng Jieh Pahng Dwei Chuck Fong Tien Wahk Gik
Eighteen-Technique Pa-Kwa Staff vs. Left-Right Thirteen Lances Spear	Sup-Bot Sik Bot-Gwa Gwun Dwei Chuck Jor-Yauh Sup-Sam Cheung
Rattan Shield and Sword vs. Diamond Trident	Dahn Do Tahn Pai Dip Dwei Chuck Gam Gong Pa
Long-Handled Two-Section Cudgel vs. Rattan Shield and Tonfa	Daaih So Ji Dwei Chuck Tahng Pai Gwai
Tiger's Head Shield and Sword vs. Kwan-Do	Dahn Do Fu Tau Pai Dwei Chuck Kwan-Do
Rattan Shield and Sword vs. Bin-Gwai Double-Ended Staff	Dahn Do Dip Dwei Chuck Seung Tau Bin Gwai Gwun
Rattan Shield and Sword vs. Horse Bench	Dahn Do Dip Dwei Chuck Cheung Kiu Dahng
Spear/Sword/Staff Three-Man Combat Set	Cheung, Gwun, Do, Sam Yun Chuck
Kwan-Do/Snake-Tongue Spear/ Double-Edged Sword vs. Fong Tien Wahk Gik	Kwan-Do, Seh Mau Cheung, Gim, Dwei Chuck Fong Tien Wahk Gik

Choy Li Fut Training Dummy Sets

Sandbag Dummy	Sah Bau Jong
Balanced Wooden Dummy	Ching Jong
Leg Dummy	Geuk Jong
Staff Dummy	Gwun Jong
Spring Dummy	Dan Wong Jong
Copper Man Dummy	Tung Yen Jong
Horse Power Dummy	Mah Lihk Jong
Bamboo Forest Dummy	Jook Lam Jong

153

About the Authors

Doc Fai Wong has been teaching choy li fut since 1969 in San Francisco, California. Besides running his kung-fu school, he teaches tai chi ch'uan for San Francisco Community College and is a California State Certified acupuncturist.

Wong studied kung-fu originally from one of choy li fut's great-grandmasters, Lau Bun, in San Francisco. After Lau Bun passed away, Wong continued his studies with Great-grand-master Woo Van Cheuk and with Grandmasters Wong Gong and Wong Ying Sum in Hong Kong. Doc Fai Wong is of the fifth generation in choy li fut lineage, making him one of the highest ranking choy li fut masters in North America.

The president of the Choy Li Fut International Federation, Wong has associate choy li fut schools located throughout the United States, and in ten cities in Spain and England.

Jane Hallander is a freelance writer of over 100 published articles, both in the United States and overseas. She is the author of *Kung Fu Fighting Styles,* and has been a practitioner of the martial arts for many years.

UNIQUE LITERARY BOOKS OF THE WORLD

Also publishers of:
Inside Karate
Inside Kung-Fu

UNIQUE PUBLICATIONS
4201 Vanowen Place
Burbank, CA 91505

PLEASE WRITE IN
FOR OUR LATEST CATALOG